A CONVERSATION WITH WISDOM

STUDENT WORKBOOK WITH TEACHER'S NOTES

BY
JOSEPH N. WILLIAMS
WITH E. E. MURDOCH

TRUE PERSPECTIVE PUBLISHING HOUSE

www.trueperspectivepublishing.com

Contents

How to Use This Workbook

This workbook consists of practical exercises to help you apply the lessons discussed in the student reader. These exercises include memory verses, multiple choice questions, short writing assignments and more. To get the most out of this workbook, look up the bracketed references and jot down important notes in the margins when necessary. Turn in assignments on time, ask questions, and prayerfully consider ways to implement these lessons in your life. It may help to print memory verses on separate index cards for easy reference.

Charge to Teachers

I hope that you are excited about teaching this course. You have been charged with the task of imparting wisdom to the students in this class, not only by teaching them the Bible and using these practical tools, but by walking in wisdom in your own life as much as possible.

This course is designed to be very practical, dealing with situations that may arise in students' lives every single day—however, there are many opportunities to go deeper with the teaching for advanced students who want a more theological, exegetically focused study. Although it is practical, it requires a good deal of at-home Bible study and in-depth workbook assignments. Students will need to prepare for the work level at the beginning of the semester.

The goal is not to turn out a class full of students who are perfect and will never make an unwise decision again in their lives—the goal is to empower them to face life's challenges knowing that there are answers in God's

word for each situation, and that no area of their lives is

considered unimportant to Him. The Holy Spirit will work

through thorny day-to-day scenarios to prune us so that we

will bear more fruit, have more faith, and grow from

strength to strength, and glory to glory in Christ Jesus.

Ultimately, learning the principles of godly wisdom is

about glorifying Him and working together, experiencing

and expanding the Kingdom of God.

This series works best if assigned one week at a

time. This way, the workbook answers can be reviewed at

the next class. In addition to the reader and workbook,

each student should have access to a good study Bible and

dictionary of Bible words. You may leave room within the

class hour for students to show that they have memorized

the assigned scriptures for that week.

When teaching, you may refer to the notes at the

back of the book for discussion points or further

explanation. Don't be unprepared! The students depend on teachers to study the lesson (and pray for illumination) beforehand. If you don't know the answer to something and it isn't provided here, don't panic. Simply tell the student you will research the answer and get back to him at the following session. Use anecdotes and illustrations to get your points across. The Lord Jesus did this often, speaking to crowds in parables. These were earthly stories with heavenly meanings that took something hard to comprehend and made it accessible to their hearts and minds.

Finally, pray for each of your students. They signed up for this course because they believed that they would receive a divine deposit that would cause them to dialogue with their destinies and fulfill their purposes in God. Lift them up and rejoice with them whenever progress is made.

Be enriched in your faith as you go forth in this series of assignments!

Foreword

Wisdom is primarily the principle thing. This workbook is a wonderful tool to express and demonstrate the importance and significance of wisdom in everything we do. Bishop Joseph N. Williams has shown in this work that wisdom is a must for successful existence, in as much as, wisdom is God's knowledge applied to worldly negotiations. It is a point of contact with reality and a catalyst for new experiences, new ideas, new people and new places. Bishop Williams has done a masterful job with this workbook that should prove to be a tool to help thousands of people. Well done, true yokefellow.

Bishop Ronald Carter

Refuge Church of Christ, Freeport, L. I.

Chapter 1

WISDOM: FIRST STEPS TO UNDERSTANDING

Using a Bible dictionary of Old Testament words, look up the words "wise" and "wisdom" as used in Gen. 3:4-6 and Prov. 9:10. What is wisdom?

_____

_____

_____

_____

_____

_____

_____

Read 1 Kings 3. Describe the relationship between extravagant worship and discovering what to do in a challenging situation.

_____

_____

_____

_____

_____

_____

Read 1 Cor. 12:8. How does the spiritual gift of wisdom operate? Discuss with group.

_____

_____

_____

_____

_____

_____

Read Proverbs 1:1-7. Explain the purposes of this biblical

book as stated in those verses. What do you learn about the

role of wisdom and instruction in a life devoted to God's

glory each day? What do you expect to gain from this

study?

_____

_____

_____

_____

_____

_____

_____

_____

Review James 3:13-18 and identify the eightfold nature of

heavenly wisdom. Commit this list to memory.

_____

_____

_____

_____

_____

_____

_____

Chapter 2

WISDOM PERSONIFIED

Read Prov. 1:20-33. What are your thoughts on this passage? What is the result of despising knowledge and instruction? Why is it so terrible to be left to one's own devices? Write a brief response to this passage and commit verse 33 to memory. Be prepared to recite it for the next class.

_____

_____

_____

_____

_____

_____

_____

_____

Read Prov. 8:1-21. Write a brief response to this passage.

What is the fear of the Lord, according to this passage?

What is durable wealth?

_____

_____

_____

_____

_____

_____

_____

_____

Search the Scriptures. Find one verse that corresponds with each statement:

a)   Wisdom comes from God Himself. Prov. _____

b)   Wisdom existed from the beginning. Prov. _____

Read Prov. 8:6-9. What are some "excellent things" spoken

by wisdom?

_____

_____

_____

_____

_____

_____

How do you see "truth" in Prov. 8:7? What is an

abomination? What does it mean to be "crooked" or

"perverse?"

_____

_____

_____

_____

_____

_____

Is loving righteousness the same as hating wickedness?

Why or why not?

_____

_____

_____

_____

_____

_____

_____

_____

Read Prov. 9:1-12. Have you ever tried to correct a scoffer or reprove a wise person? If so, what was the result of that encounter? Write a short response to these verses, including a note about your experience. Identify three benefits of wisdom.

_____

_____

_____

_____

_____

_____

_____

_____

Read Prov. 9:13-18. What does this mean to you? Write about a time in life when Folly called out to you and you refused to listen. If you did listen, write about the consequences of engaging in something unwise, and what you learned from it.

_____

_____

_____

_____

_____

_____

_____

_____

Read Prov. 7:6-23. Why is the young man in this illustration compared to an ox headed for slaughter? What can we learn from this passage about being in the wrong place at the wrong time?

_____

_____

_____

_____

_____

_____

_____

_____

Read Section 2.8. Are there any areas on the list that you

know need improvement in your life? Are you prepared to

be renewed in your mind in those areas? What changes can

you make to reflect this? Do not share with the class—it is

for personal reference.

_____

_____

_____

_____

_____

_____

_____

Chapter 3

FOUR TYPES OF FOOLS

Write about the mercy of God in turning the foolish away

from folly and bringing their hearts to a place of wisdom

and communion with Him. In what ways have your

experiences with the Lord made you wiser to the schemes

of the enemy to thwart your destiny in God?

_____

_____

_____

_____

_____

_____

_____

_____

Write about the snare of gullibility and how these verses
can help you to guard against it.

_____

_____

_____

_____

_____

_____

_____

_____

Search the Scriptures. Find an example of someone who refused to listen to rebuke and suffered for it. Find an example of someone who embraced correction and responded to it correctly, ultimately becoming wiser for it. Discuss with group.

_____

_____

_____

_____

_____

_____

_____

_____

Explain how we should respond to those who scoff at
(attempt to make a mockery of) the claims of the gospel.
What do you think is meant by the phrase "God is not
mocked"?

_____

_____

_____

_____

_____

_____

_____

_____

Read James 4:6-10. What is the biblical remedy for an

arrogant attitude? Why is boasting and self-seeking

incompatible with wisdom? What is the root of this

attitude?

_____

_____

_____

_____

_____

Explain how humility and submission can guard us from a

rebellious attitude. In keeping with Jesus' teaching in Matt.

5:22, why is it wrong to call people "worthless" or "fool"?

_____

_____

_____

_____

_____

After breaking up into small groups, come up with a five minute skit that illustrates the behavior of one type of fool. Focus on poor choices and their consequences. Each skit must also illustrate the path of wisdom taken in the same situation. Make the connection between the lesson and how we should govern ourselves as Christians walking wisely in today's world.

_____

_____

_____

_____

_____

_____

_____

_____

Chapter 4

CHOOSING WHAT'S BETTER

Read Prov. 3:13-18. Identify five characteristics or benefits of wisdom within the passage.

_____

_____

_____

_____

_____

_____

_____

_____

Memorize Prov. 15:16. Rephrase this proverb in your own

words.

_____

_____

_____

_____

_____

Memorize Prov. 15:17. What does this scripture mean to

you?

_____

_____

_____

_____

_____

_____

Memorize Prov. 16:32. With this principle in mind, write about why some young people are so angry today. Do you think there is ever a good reason to be angry with God? Complete this sentence: "Controlling my temper means I must..."

_____

_____

_____

_____

_____

_____

_____

_____

Memorize Prov. 16:19. Why do you think this is true?

_____

_____

_____

_____

_____

_____

Memorize Prov. 28:6. Explain.

_____

_____

_____

_____

_____

_____

_____

Memorize Prov. 27:5-6. Write about a time when you

experienced the wound of a friend or the kiss of an enemy.

How did you respond? Do not share with the class. This is

for your reference.

_____

_____

_____

_____

_____

_____

_____

_____

Write a short paragraph on the difference between

correction (which teaches us to do things the right way) and

perfection (which aims to produce another level of

maturity) in God's dealings with His people.

_____

_____

_____

_____

_____

_____

_____

_____

Fill in the blanks. The first verse has been completed as an

example. Rephrase each verse in your own words.

REFERENCE	BETTER IS...	THAN...
Prov. 12:9	He that is lightly esteemed, and hath a servant	he that honoreth himself, and lacketh bread
Prov. 19:1		
Prov. 21:19		
Prov. 25:7		
Prov. 27:10		

Chapter 5

SETTING AND MAINTAINING WISE

BOUNDARIES

Memorize Prov. 22:3. How does removing yourself from

evil associations and environments help your walk with

God? How does it help physically, emotionally, and

spiritually? In what ways can you limit bad influences or

associations?

_____

_____

_____

_____

_____

_____

_____

There are three areas in which we must know God's will and demonic set-ups. They are: 1) social pressure, 2) sexual pressure, and 3) emotional imbalance. Write about how one of these areas affects you. Find at least one scripture containing a warning about that area and memorize it. Do not hand this in. It is for your reference.

_____

_____

_____

_____

_____

_____

_____

Reread 1 Cor. 5:9-13. What is the main point of emphasis here? "Not to company with" is strong language. How do you interpret this?

_____

_____

_____

_____

_____

_____

_____

_____

Read 2 Cor. 7:1, 10-11. Write it out in your own words.

Can you identify the seven fruits of repentance in the above

passage? Write two paragraphs describing how you might

put the preceding lesson into practice in your life.

_____

_____

_____

_____

_____

_____

_____

Chapter 6

WISDOM AT WORK

What is the purpose of work? Discuss in class. Pray for the work of everyone's hands to be blessed; pray for favor on jobs; pray for new careers or training avenues for those who are currently seeking employment. Pray for increased power to be salt and light at work, and for the salvation of coworkers and managers.

_____

_____

_____

_____

_____

_____

_____

What are your thoughts on the slothful spirit? How can a

renewed mindset cancel a slothful outlook?

_____

_____

_____

_____

_____

Using a Bible dictionary of Old and New Testament words,

look up the words "slothful" and "diligence" as used in

Prov. 12:24 and 2 Pet. 1:5. What are your thoughts?

_____

_____

_____

_____

_____

Write two paragraphs about your work ethic. Are you diligent? Are you slothful? Pray about areas where you have been challenged. Have faith in the grace and power of God to meet your needs.

_____

_____

_____

_____

_____

_____

_____

_____

Tap into your arsenal of gifts and talents. Are you able to do something that is both God-glorifying and profitable? Seek God as to whether you can develop those skills into a business. Do you see someone with a skill or talent they do not appear to be using? Encourage them! Some of us just need a little push before we can dream big.

_____

_____

_____

_____

_____

_____

Chapter 7

ECCLESIASTES: THE SEARCH FOR LIFE'S

MEANING

Review the following well-known sayings from the book of

Ecclesiastes:

a)   Eccles. 1:9

b)   Eccles. 1:10

c)   Eccles. 3:1

d)   Eccles. 12:1

e)   Eccles. 12:13

How do these verses shape or express your view of human life?

_____

_____

_____

_____

_____

_____

Read Eccles. 1:3-11 and determine why nothing makes sense without God. Write a paragraph explaining this.

_____

_____

_____

_____

_____

_____

In Eccles. 2:1-11, Solomon speaks about "me, myself, and I." What is he really saying? Write a short essay explaining how such pursuits have affected your life. What have you learned about their value in the vast scheme of things?

_____

_____

_____

_____

_____

_____

_____

_____

How do you describe vanity? What is the conclusion of the whole matter? Read Eccles. 2:20-24. What is Solomon's short term attitude toward pleasure? What is his long term attitude toward work? What is God's gift to us in v. 24?

_____

_____

_____

_____

_____

_____

_____

Choose five things from Eccles. 3:1-8 that have taught you important lessons so far. Read Eccles. 3:14-15 again. You need to understand that your future has already happened! Why does God arrange life this way? Does this mean that we no longer have responsibilities in life?

_____

_____

_____

_____

_____

_____

_____

_____

In what ways have you broken out of the mold of what

people have been doing for generations?

_____

_____

_____

_____

_____

_____

What have you done that will have significance beyond

your training and death?

_____

_____

_____

_____

_____

What really motivates you to continue the daily patterns of

church, work, home and relationships?

_____

_____

_____

_____

_____

_____

What rewards do you expect from your labor?

_____

_____

_____

_____

_____

_____

_____

Chapter 8

PRINCIPLES OF FINANCIAL WISDOM

Allow this lesson to challenge you. If you do not give, start giving today. If you do not tithe, learn be faithful in this area. (1 Cor. 4:2) If you tithe, but could increase your offering, seek the Lord for increased faith to do so. Do you share what you have with those in need? If not, look around your life and prayerfully consider how you might help someone financially or materially. Perhaps you are in a good position financially and can underwrite a struggling ministry or charitable organization. Take these things to prayer and make notes for your personal reference. If you're already doing these things, just give God praise for the privilege of stewardship. Memorize Prov. 3:9-10.

What is your financial "action plan?" Do you have a budget? If not, try starting on one today. If you are in financial straits, don't despair. There is hope! He is Jehovah-Jireh, your provider.

_____

_____

_____

_____

_____

_____

_____

_____

What are some of the wrong ways you have thought about money? Think carefully about the references for each point in Section 8.2. How has your particular culture or family structure informed the ways you think about your finances? Begin to seek God for a breakthrough in areas that pose particular challenges. Mediate on Psalm 49.

_____

_____

_____

_____

_____

_____

_____

_____

Think positively about finances, believing that God is able to bless you in this area. Revisit your individual or family budget. How much is spent on entertainment? Junk food? Cell phone and text messaging costs? Is there something you can reduce or cut in order to either a) save something; b) give something; or c) invest something? Write two paragraphs about your considerations.

_____

_____

_____

_____

_____

_____

_____

Read the references provided in Section 8.4. What lessons

do you learn from the ant? Do you have sound financial

advisors in your life? Are you overworking just so you can

have more stuff? Do you save money or are you living

from check to check?

_____

_____

_____

_____

_____

_____

_____

_____

Write about the sin of showing partiality because of wealth.
How do you think the Lord feels when He sees this attitude
among His children?

_____

_____

_____

_____

_____

_____

_____

_____

If you are a business owner or manager, do you make sure

that your employees receive fair pay for their work? Make

any challenges in this lesson a matter for prayer.

_____

_____

_____

_____

_____

_____

_____

Go through your closet and determine to give one item away to someone less fortunate. Instead of choosing something well-worn (though it may be in good condition), or something that no longer appeals to you, choose an outfit that is your favorite, best, or most costly, and let it go. Write a short testimony about this experience. Memorize Acts 20:35.

_____

_____

_____

_____

_____

_____

_____

Chapter 9

FACING LIFE'S CHALLENGES

Read Psalm 90. Take a few moments and reflect on the brevity of life and the importance of redeeming (buying back at one's expense) the time we are given. Are you using your time wisely? If not, what changes can you make to show your acceptance of Moses' attitude toward time?

_____

_____

_____

_____

_____

_____

_____

Fill in the blanks on the following chart. Two have already been completed as examples. For each principle, write whether it relates to knowing "how," "when," or "what" to do. What do you learn from thinking through everyday choices in this manner?

_____

_____

_____

_____

_____

_____

_____

THINKING THINGS THROUGH

Scripture Reference	Seed, Cause, or Action	Fruit, Effect, or Result	In Your Own Words
Prov. 24:10	Little strength	Fainting in the day of adversity	
Prov. 24:17-18	Don't rejoice when your enemy falls or is overthrown	It displeases the Lord, who may remove His anger from him	
Prov. 24:27	First prepare your work in the field	Then go and build your house	
Prov. 25:8	Don't be in a hurry to stir up strife	You won't know what do when your neighbor embarrasses you	Don't be quick to start a fight.

Prov. 25:20	Don't sing to a heavy heart	It's like taking away someone's coat in winter	
Gal. 6:9	Don't be weary in well doing. If you don't faint	In due season you will reap	

Define the following terms: foresight; insight; hindsight.

How have you learned from these?

_____

_____

_____

_____

_____

_____

_____

We can learn to face the realities of life effectively. Read

Heb. 4:14-16. What are your thoughts on the availability of

well-timed help? Explain.

_____

_____

_____

_____

_____

_____

What are some life challenges that you try to:

a)   Escape?

_____

_____

_____

_____

b)   Deny?

_____

_____

_____

_____

c)   Handle with indifference?

_____

_____

_____

_____

How will you handle them differently as a result of this

lesson?

_____

_____

_____

_____

_____

Chapter 10

SELECTING YOUR CABINET

Read Eccles. 4:12. Explain in your own words. Write two paragraphs about a time when you were tempted to go into isolation and how you came out of it.

_____

_____

_____

_____

_____

_____

_____

Write a short letter to your children (or someone else's) teaching them how to do choose their friends at school. Do not send the letter, it is for your reference.

_____

_____

_____

_____

_____

_____

Read Prov. 9:9. Write it out. What does this mean to you? How do you select advisers and evaluate what they have to say?

_____

_____

_____

_____

_____

Do you surround yourself with people who know more than you do in certain areas, or do you only associate with those who know what you know? Why or why not? Why is important to broaden your circle?

_____

_____

_____

_____

_____

_____

_____

_____

Chapter 11

LINKING OUR GOALS TO GOD'S PURPOSE

Read 3:14. At first glance it may seem to suggest that

nothing people do really matters. As if God's will is

ultimately going to be done and nothing may be added to it

or taken away. So why not just wait for Him to do

everything?

_____

_____

_____

_____

_____

_____

_____

Write down some of your goals, dreams, and skills. Which
of these are your own ideas, and which are you certain fit
into God's plan for your life in the near or distant future?
How does Ecclesiastes invite you to link your goals with
God's designs? Why does God call us to personal
relationship with Him?

_____

_____

_____

_____

_____

_____

_____

Name five things to place value upon while maturing in the things of God.

a)   Proverbs 15:16

b)   Proverbs 16:8

c)   Proverbs 16: 19

d)   Proverbs 17:1

e)   Proverbs 28:6

Prayerfully fill out the Abilities Chart in Appendix 1.

Read Joshua 1:8. What is "good success?"

_____

_____

_____

_____

_____

_____

Name three ways we can participate with God in our own

spiritual development.

_____

_____

_____

_____

_____

_____

_____

Chapter 12

THE ART OF SPEAKING WISELY

Write two short paragraphs about a time when you said
something you wish you could take back. Though you
cannot take words back after they are spoken, what else
should you do if you are able?

_____

_____

_____

_____

_____

_____

_____

Write about the value of an encouraging word given at a time of need.

_____

_____

_____

_____

_____

We always hear Proverbs 18:21 quoted. What does it really mean?

_____

_____

_____

_____

_____

_____

God wants us to bless our enemies, not curse them. (Rom.

12:14) Why do you think He tells us to do this?

_____

_____

_____

_____

_____

_____

_____

_____

Our words reveal what is present in our hearts. What do
your words reveal about you? Do not hand this in, it is for
your reference.

_____

_____

_____

_____

_____

_____

_____

Chapter 13

MAKING IT PERSONAL

<u>Final Review</u>

1.   What is the fear of the Lord and why is it so

important to our discussion of wisdom?

_____

_____

_____

_____

_____

_____

_____

2.   Wisdom is likened to a woman crying aloud to

people in the street. What is she saying?

_____

_____

_____

_____

_____

_____

3.   Name the four types of fools and give one

characteristic of each.

_____

_____

_____

_____

_____

_____

4.   Why is delayed glory better than instant

gratification?

_____

_____

_____

_____

_____

_____

5.   What is prudence? Name two people in scripture

who kept good company.

_____

_____

_____

_____

_____

_____

_____

6.   Why is good work ethic important? Why do human

beings work? How does laziness lead to lack?

_____

_____

_____

_____

_____

_____

7.   What lesson did Solomon learn from pursuing all

the best that life had to offer? What was his conclusion?

_____

_____

_____

_____

_____

_____

8.   What is stewardship? Why is favor with God better

than money?

_____

_____

_____

_____

_____

_____

_____

9.   What should our attitude be toward planning for tomorrow? Name two ways we may face life's challenges effectively.

_____

_____

_____

_____

_____

_____

10.   Why are advisers necessary?

_____

_____

_____

_____

_____

_____

11.   If God knows everything, why can't we just sit back
and wait for Him to do everything for us?

_____

_____

_____

_____

_____

_____

_____

12.   Name five characteristics of wise, godly speech.

_____

_____

_____

_____

_____

_____

GENERAL QUESTIONS

13.   My relationship with God is:

a)   A source of frustration

b)   Characterized by seeking Him

c)   Weak in the face of trouble

d)   In need of a change (if so, what change?)

_____

_____

_____

_____

_____

_____

_____

_____

14.   Write out John 14:26.

_____

_____

_____

_____

_____

_____

_____

_____

15.   Fill in the terms that correspond to each statement.

a)   God is all knowing. (   )

b)   God is everywhere. (   )

c)   God is all powerful. (   )

16.   Complete each sentence:

a)   He can enable me to accomplish anything. I would like to…

_____

_____

_____

_____

_____

_____

b)   He is always present with me. This assures me because…

_____

_____

_____

_____

_____

17.   Joining and staying with Jesus requires major

adjustment! Read Luke 9:23-24. How do you see it?

_____

_____

_____

_____

_____

_____

_____

18.　　What kinds of adjustments have you had to make in the following areas?

a)　　Responding to Difficult Circumstances

_____

_____

_____

_____

_____

_____

b)　　Relationships

_____

_____

_____

_____

_____

_____

_____

_____

c)   Actions/Overall Behavior

_____

_____

_____

_____

_____

_____

_____

_____

d)   Thought life

_____

_____

_____

_____

_____

_____

_____

e)   Commitments to God, to Others, to Self

_____

_____

_____

_____

_____

_____

_____

f)   Beliefs

_____

_____

_____

_____

_____

_____

_____

19.   What is meant by "my personal responsibility

within limits?"

_____

_____

_____

_____

_____

_____

_____

20.	How do you feel when you must say "no" to

something or someone?

_____

_____

_____

_____

_____

_____

_____

_____

20a.	Read Matt. 18:8-9. What was Jesus actually saying?

_____

_____

_____

_____

_____

_____

21.   Psalm 119:2 teaches me…

_____

_____

_____

_____

_____

_____

_____

_____

22.   In Prov. 22:3 I learn to keep it together by…

_____

_____

_____

_____

_____

_____

_____

_____

23.   I must choose my friends wisely because…

_____

_____

_____

_____

_____

_____

_____

Chapter 1 Teacher's Notes

1) The eight (8) characteristics of godly wisdom in James 3:13-18 are: purity, peaceableness, gentleness, approachability (easy to speak to), mercy, good fruits, impartiality (not showing favoritism), and sincerity (no hypocrisy).

2) Discuss the story of Solomon's request for wisdom (1 Kings 3) in more detail, in particular the concept that worship encounters often lead to the release of information to aid the worshipper in their current or next assignment.

3) Discuss the role of wise men in the courts of biblical kings and leaders. Highlight special occasions when God used righteous men, such as Daniel and Joseph, to interpret dreams or give prophetic guidance to leaders, resulting great deliverance.

4) Explain that this book covers advanced theological themes in a brief, general manner. Students interested in further study may refer to these notes.

5) Expand on the connection between the power of the Holy Spirit and the expression of wisdom in times of conflict. Discuss it from the perspective of Christian apologetics (the defense the faith), as well as daily dealings with personal or spiritual enemies. Explain that for something as simple as serving widows in the daily allowance, anointing and wisdom were required. (Acts 6:3)

Chapter 2 Teacher's Notes

1) Paul goes into detail about God's wisdom and power in 1 Corinthians 1:17-31. Engage the class in a discussion on some differences between worldly wisdom and spiritual wisdom.

2) Challenge students to examine the list of Notable Lessons closely and pray about those areas which need improvement.

3) To bring this lesson forward to the New Testament, open a discussion about Jesus' parable of the Wise and Foolish Builders or the parable of the Wise and Foolish Virgins. (Matt. 7:21-29; Matt 25:1-13)

Chapter 3 Teacher's Notes

1) Folly and pride are related. Discuss the first mention of pride as it relates to the fall of Lucifer in Isaiah 14:12-15. A thorough review of his "I will" statements and subsequent eviction from heaven should accentuate this lesson for more advanced students.

2) Discuss King Saul's failure to execute the Amalekites as God commanded in 1 Samuel 15. Explore the connections between pride and folly, paying particular attention to how Saul answered when questioned by Samuel. Note that partial obedience is still disobedience, and how Saul was more concerned about saving his reputation than glorifying God. His repentance was not genuine, but self-serving, and a show for the public.

3) Address the state of man before regeneration and how that rebellion is brought to an end in Christ, using the conversion of Saul of Tarsus (Paul) as a starting point. (Acts 9:1-18)

4) Explain why, although we may recognize folly in others, we are not to refer to others as "fools" in a derogatory manner. (Prov. 10:18; Mat. 5:22)

Chapter 4 Teacher's Notes

1) Emphasize to the class that although God is sovereign and works all things according to the counsel of His own will; He yet requires our obedience and holds us responsible for the choices we make. Through the Word of God and the Spirit of God, He gives us all the tools we need to make decisions that will glorify Him—to place a high premium not just on what is good, but what is better and best in this life.

2) Demonstrate that when they are faced with challenges in daily life, they can refer back to the principles of what is better, and so can know what to do. How do we handle situations in life for which there is no specific scripture?

3) Pray with the class that they will make better life choices after this lesson and break the cycles that keep them from making true progress.

4) For students desiring deeper study, point them to the book of Hebrews for a discussion of the Better Covenant; Better Promises; Better Hope; Better Resurrection, *et al.* See also Paul's desire to depart to be with Christ (which was better) versus remaining on earth which was needful. (Phil. 1:23)

5) Caution against hastiness in spiritual and relational matters. One may be zealous to preach when they have not attained to spiritual maturity. Perhaps they are truly called to do this, but they have to be trained, prepared, and sent - not just by life experience, but also by diligent study of the Word of God. This takes time - with zeal there is a tendency to want everything "right now." Major life decisions are also to be entered into with wise counsel, prayer and forethought.

Chapter 5 Teacher's Notes

1) It may be good to discuss the man who was expelled from the Corinthian church (1 Cor. 5:1-13), as well as the error of refusing to forgive and restore the brother once he repented of his wrongdoing. Note that separation from bad company in the world is a given, but that this portion addresses separation from professing believers living in sin.

2) Discuss the attitude of the older brother in the parable of the Prodigal Son. (Luke 15:11-32)

3) Show that wisdom will let you know the timing and procedure for such separations.

4) The seven fruits of repentance listed in 2 Cor. 7:10-11 are carefulness; clearing of oneself; indignation; fear; vehement desire; zeal; and vengeance.

Chapter 6 Teacher's Notes

1) Impress on students that being a Christian does not mean that you won't have to work for a living, necessarily. Encourage good work habits and career advancement where God's glory is clearly in view.

2) Explain that while diligence brings reward, we should not overwork to be rich. This is not balance.

3) Encourage mothers who, instead of working, stay at home with their children. They are neither lazy nor unproductive, but in fact working to invest in young lives, training them up in righteousness.

4) Some people cannot find employment. Encourage students to share knowledge of new opportunities with each other; or to make their skills available to help others get on their feet professionally.

Chapter 7 Teacher's Notes

1)   Review the list of Solomon's pursuits with the class and explain that without God at the center of one's life, any gains in life appear to be futile, fleeting and unfulfilling. The lesson should encourage them to seek God first, follow His principles for living, and not develop a cynical or fatalistic view of human existence.

2)   Explain the differences between two outlooks: the one that says "get all you can before you die" and the one that says, "fear God and keep His commandments." Explain that eternal perspective is necessary in order to have a correct judgment of things.

3)   Expound here on the impact of the Fall on the entire cycle of life, including the earth itself.

Chapter 8 Teacher's Notes

1) The goal of this lesson is to have the students examine their current beliefs and practices in regards to finances and, if changes need to be made, to encourage them in acts of faith. Explain to students that money is neither evil nor good, but necessary, and that giving is an active, vital part of their worship.

2) Explain that wealth alone is not an indicator of blessing - because there are plenty of wicked persons with abundant financial resources and possessions. However, durable riches and wealth dwell with true, godly wisdom, and if we follow the principles of Scripture, we will not do without. On the other hand, God allows the wicked to store up such wealth, so He can take it away and give it to those who please Him. (Eccles. 2:26)

3) Pray with the class that the psychological stronghold of poverty—an oppressed mindset—will be broken off of their lives, and the lives of their families; pray that God will give them hearts abounding with loving generosity - and bring forth those who will cheerfully sow into the Kingdom of God. Discuss the difference between actual oppression and having an oppressed mindset.

4) Emphasize the importance of staying out of debt and paying bills on time; and rebuke laziness in the sense that some believe they don't need to have a job (or own a business), but that money will just come to them because they are spiritual.

5) For those who want further study, point them to Paul's teaching in 2 Corinthians 8-9 regarding sowing and reaping; seedtime and harvest; and other kingdom principles about financial increase. Remind them that they should "prosper and be in health, even as their soul prospers." (3 Jn. 1:2)

6) Some students may have questions not covered in this lesson. They may ask: What if I am married and my spouse refuses to consent to tithing/ or is not a believer? What if I am living on a fixed income, and need every dollar I have? What can I give to God if I have no income at the present time? What about gambling? What does the Bible say about claiming bankruptcy? Be prepared to answer difficult questions.

7) Discuss the miraculous power of God to provide for His children.

Chapter 9 Teacher's Notes

1) Try to communicate to students the value of time as a perishable resource and why we must use it to God's glory. Encourage students to develop a schedule to determine how they spend their time and whether it reflects proper priorities. Create a hypothetical weekly schedule with the class—list all of the activities that could and should fill it, taking suggestions from the group. Then look for items that can be cut, reduced, postponed, or added to be more efficient in pursuing God's will in this fictitious person's life.

2) The topic of divine timing can be expanded by tracing biblical characters movements in relation to a prophetic word, as in the cases of Esther or Cyrus; or by selecting specific moments when key events coincided, as with the feast of Pentecost and the birth of the church. In the case of Joseph (Jacob's son), observe how he was positioned in the

right place at the right time, equipped with the wisdom to do what was necessary. Compare this to the church today, and those who are gifted with wisdom and discernment.

3) Remind students that wisdom is available to us for the asking.

4) Explain the concept of psychological warfare.

Chapter 10 Teacher's Notes

1) Everyone needs counselors and friendships. Explain the characteristics of each and why it's important to choose wisely regarding these. Use examples of solid friendships, such as Naomi and Ruth, or Jonathan and David. (See Ruth 1:6-18; 1 Sam. 20:1-42)

2) Christianity is rooted in community and involvement. Emphasize the spiritual family relationships shared by believers, and explain how we can help one another overcome obstacles in our walks with God by giving practical, real-life examples.

3) Explain that God sometimes allows people to move into and out of our lives in order to propel us toward our destinies in Him. There is a reason for the shifting. Discuss the fact that sometimes God will not allow people to help us in a situation because He is teaching us to depend on Him alone.

Chapter 11 Teacher's Notes

1) Connect this lesson to discovering God's purpose in the student's lives. Show them that their goals must become God's goals if they are to prosper. Explain that obedience supersedes any sacrifices they can make.

2) Help students take stock of their skills, natural abilities and spiritual gifts using the abilities chart in Appendix 1. Encourage them to serve in church in some capacity, to grow in areas to which they have been called, and to submit to the Lord for the preparatory process that may be required.

Chapter 12 Teacher's Notes

1) Emphasize to students that the way we speak to God, to others, and even to ourselves is of critical importance to our everyday life. We can speak either death or life, faith or doubt. (Prov. 18:21; Matt. 12:36; 2 Cor. 4:13)

2) Students interested in further study may be interested to know that in the days of the Old Testament, women made vows unto God but their husbands or fathers had the right to break those vows if they felt it could not or should not be fulfilled. (Num. 30)

3) Discuss with the class different ways they can speak up for the cause of the oppressed or speak out against injustice in their communities, city, nation, or on the international level.

Chapter 13 Teacher's Notes

1) Since the answers to some questions may be sensitive in nature, this review should not be handed in, although it may be presented to the instructor for credit. You may substitute or add questions for advanced students in this final review section. If they would like to share what they learned in addition to the course curriculum, this may be a good means of doing so. The important thing is to encourage everyone to live a life governed by godly wisdom with the help of the Holy Spirit.

Appendix 1

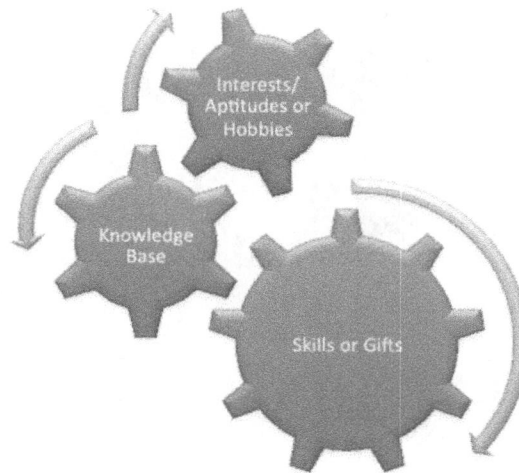

1) What are your interests, aptitudes or hobbies? These are things you enjoy doing, are good at, or do on the side when you have time. Have you pursued them? Why or why not?

2) What is your knowledge base? This includes formal education as well as life experience.

3) What are your skills? This includes work experience, trades, or anything learned formally, such as an instrument.

4) What are your gifts? These are spiritual enablements given to you by the Holy Spirit for the benefit of the Body of Christ.

www.ingramcontent.com/pod-product-compliance
Lightning Source LLC
Chambersburg PA
CBHW081514040426
42447CB00013B/3217